WINNING
MORE
THAN THE GAME

DEVELOPING CHARACTER THROUGH SPORTS

Written by
Athletes for a Better World

Winning More Than The Game

ISBN: 9798844014475

ATHLETES
FOR A BETTER
WORLD

Winning More Than The Game

(www.abw.org)

Founded in 1998, the mission of Athletes for a Better World (ABW) is to use sports to develop character, teamwork, and citizenship through commitment to an athletic *Code for Living* that applies to life, and to create a movement that will play a significant role in the transformation of individuals, sports, and society. This mission is accomplished through creation of curricula to teach character formation, and then to recognize athletic character through award and scholarship programs.

Athletes for a Better World is a 501(c)(3) nonprofit organization.

THE CODE FOR LIVING
Life Lessons Learned through Sports

Because I am a role model and have the opportunity and responsibility to make a difference in the lives of others, I commit to this Code. I will take responsibility and appropriate actions when I fail to live up to it.

AS AN INDIVIDUAL:

- I will develop my skills to the best of my ability and give my best effort in practice and competition.
- I will compete within the spirit and letter of the rules of my sport.
- I will respect the dignity of every human being, and will not be abusive or dehumanizing of anyone either as an athlete or as a fan.

AS A MEMBER OF A TEAM:

- I will place team goals ahead of personal goals.
- I will be a positive influence on the relationships on the team.
- I will follow the team rules established by the coach.

AS A MEMBER OF SOCIETY:

- I will display caring and honorable behavior off the field and be a positive influence in my community and world.
- I will give of my time, skills, and money as I am able for the betterment of my community and world.

Foreword
by Josh King

Each day we wake up to an incredible opportunity. An opportunity to improve who we are as a person. An opportunity to be a better teammate. An opportunity to make the world a better place. What matters upon opening our eyes in the morning, is what we consciously choose to do with this opportunity that has been presented to us.

The ABW *Code for Living* equips us with the framework to improve as an individual, teammate, and member of society. In my life, sports have truly enhanced my ability in each of the components mentioned above. Most importantly, I am forever thankful for the teachings of my parents -- Sheridan and Lawrence and what they instilled in me that provided the guidance I needed to create my own path and code for living. They exemplified the concept of treating everyone with respect and dignity. It is foundational in our family to judge a person solely on the content of their character, not by any external attributes or characteristics. Synonymous with the *Code for Living*, I have always been taught to strive to be the best version of myself and to consciously put team goals ahead of my own. "We, over me" has been a way of life since my first year of organized sports.

Winning More Than The Game has workbook exercises that provide active steps on enhancing your individual craft. Throughout each chapter, the book proposes questions that allow you to analyze the composition of your character and conduct more thorough introspection. I use this character development playbook to align my values with my actions. Journaling in conjunction with reading *Winning More Than The Game* heightens the sense of responsibility to myself, my team, and my community.

If you are reading this, you are likely an athlete, parent, coach, or a form of an athletic administrator. At the foundation of all of these titles is the same descriptor. We are all human beings. We can use our inherent compassion and drive to commit to the ABW *Code for Living* to add meaningful value to our lives, teams, and communities.

Through your purchase of this book, you are helping to make the world a better place. My portion of the proceeds will go to the charity of my choice — Boys & Girls Clubs of America. The money will aid America's well-deserving youth in reaching their full potential as productive, caring, and responsible citizens.

I encourage you to join me in making a commitment to yourself, your team, and your community.

Joshua King

JOSH KING
Profile in Character

ACADEMICS/INSTITUTIONAL
United States Merchant Marine Academy Class of 2022
Major: Marine Engineering and Shipyard Management
GPA: 3.70 - Magna Cum Laude Honors
U.S. Coast Guard 3rd Assistant Engineer, Unlimited Tonnage License
Commission: Accepted a Commission into the United States Coast Guard
Leadership Position: Regimental Commander
Awards:

- The Walter A. Kaminski Character Award
- New York Commandery, Naval Order of The United States Award
- The Thomas LeBlanc Award, Outstanding Male Senior Scholar-Athlete

ATHLETICS
Team Captain of the *Winningest Team in USMMA Football Program History*
Second Team All-Conference Linebacker
Awards:

- National Football Foundation William V. Campbell Trophy Finalist, 2022
- The Coach Wooden Citizenship Cup Collegiate Recipient, 2022

CITIZENSHIP
Solo-Organizer for a March Against Social Injustice, Summer 2020 - Haymarket, VA
Brunch of Hope (Anti-Racism event) Guest Speaker, Summer 2021- Haymarket, VA
The National Academies of Sciences Engineering and Medicine Transportation - Research Board Guest Panelist, April 2022

National Advocate Credentialing Program (NACP) Provisional
    Victim Advocate
Applied Suicide Intervention Skills Training (ASIST) Certified
USMMA Campus Culture Committee Co-Chair
USMMA Cultural Diversity Club Vice President
USMMA Student-Athlete Advisory Committee President

Coach John Wooden
and the
Coach Wooden Citizenship Cup

John Wooden, who won ten national championships during the years 1964-1975 as basketball coach at UCLA, is commonly regarded as the greatest college coach of any sport who ever lived. Universally regarded as one of the finest human beings to ever grace the world of sports, his character, conduct and selfless gifts stand at the highest level by any standard.

When Coach Wooden learned about Athletes for a Better World, he gave authorization to attach his name to an annual award, and he attended and addressed the inaugural event in Los Angeles in 2005. In his honor, the Coach Wooden Citizenship Cup is presented to six distinguished athletes, one male and one female from three divisions: two Professional or Olympic, two Collegiate, and two from the American High Schools. This award is the highest given in sports because it is open to all athletes in all sports, and because it is given not for athletic superiority, but for those athletes who achieve the highest standards of character, leadership, and citizenship. Past Cup recipients include Peyton Manning, Jackie Joyner-Kersee, Cal Ripken, Jr., Pat Summitt, Tim Tebow, Jack Nicklaus, Shannon Miller, and Drew Brees among others.

Coach Vince Dooley
and the
Vincent J. Dooley Awards & Scholarships program

"This book will further spread the value and lessons of the Code for Living to all athletes, at all levels, for many lifetimes to come. These positive role model principles summarize the athlete's responsibility as an individual, as a member of a team, and as a member of society. It is a treasured gift."
— Coach Vince Dooley

Vince Dooley has been the recipient of countless awards, including the highest national awards in coaching and in athletic administration including the Bear Bryant Lifetime Achievement Award, the Amos Alonzo Stagg Award, the Duffy Daugherty Memorial Award, the James J. Corbett Memorial Award, the John L. Toner Award, and the Homer Rice Award. He is the only person ever to hold the presidency of both the American Football Coaches Association and the National Association of Collegiate Directors of Athletics, and the only person inducted into the Sports Hall of Fame in two states, Georgia and Alabama. He was twice named NCAA National Coach of the Year, SEC Coach of the Year seven times, and NCAA District Coach of the Year six times. His football legacy was completed with his election to the National College Football Hall of Fame.

Dooley is Board Director Emeritus of Athletes for a Better World, and Chairman of the Vincent J. Dooley Awards & Scholarships program begun in 2008. The Dooley Awards are presented to one male and one female athlete in every high school in the state of Georgia for excellence on and off the field while mirroring the Code for Living. All award recipients are considered for the statewide scholarships that are conferred upon one male and one female athlete each year. Additional funding is provided to charities selected by the two scholarship recipients.

National Interscholastic Athletic Administrators Association

Dear Friends,

The National Interscholastic Athletic Administrators Association (NIAAA) is a professional organization dedicated to the promotion and facilitation of interscholastic athletics in the educational system that is vital to young people. In addition, the NIAAA is the primary provider of services and education for athletic administrators who conduct these programs. The benefits of participation opportunities for student-athletes are immeasurable for their growth and development into adulthood.

Likewise, Athletes for a Better World (ABW) was formed to utilize sports as a developer of character, teamwork, and citizenship through commitment to a *Code for Living* application for life. The NIAAA is pleased to join with ABW to provide *Winning More Than The Game* to administrators, coaches, parents, students, and supporters of high school athletics across the country.

The NIAAA Student Scholarship/Essay competition recognizes distinguished high school student athletes in the attribute areas of scholastics, leadership, citizenship, participation, volunteerism and the importance of school sports participation in the student's life. *The Code for Living* criteria have been incorporated into the scholarship application by asking applicants to reflect upon the tenets of life lessons learned through sport and how they relate and impact their life. This book challenges readers to consider the *Code for Living* via exercises, as a springboard for life qualities of character development.

The NIAAA and ABW partnership includes annually recognizing one male and one female national NIAAA scholarship winner as automatic recipients of the prestigious Coach Wooden Citizenship Cup. These two high school athletes will join two collegiate winners and two professional recipients each year as exemplary role models of the *Code for Living*. Please join us in supporting education-based athletic programs. May each of us recognize the responsibility to support young people in their learning, development and participation; commit to personally reflect the same qualities and to always share the best attributes afforded youth development through athletics.

Sincerely,

Bruce Whitehead, CMAA
NIAAA Executive Director

ENDORSEMENTS FOR THE CODE FOR LIVING...

"Sport is only a part of our lives. The Code for Living isn't just good for those of us who are professional athletes; it's good for kids of all ages and their parents."
  – Peyton Manning, NFL Hall of Fame

"We believe that there are many life lessons that can be learned through sports, and that, when taught properly, sports can help us grow on and off the field. Winning More Than The Game and its Code for Living are valuable for athletes, coaches, and parents, and ABW's mission to make everyone stronger through sports is one we can all learn from."
  – Cal Ripken, Jr., Baseball Hall of Fame

"ABW is working to create the proper values and environment in sports for our young people to grow up in. The Code for Living is needed at every level of sports today."
  – Tom Glavine, Baseball Hall of Fame

Who will benefit from reading Winning More Than the Game?

- Amateur and professional athletes
- Parents, guardians and mentors
- Sports-management students
- Sports agents
- Participants in character education or life-skills courses
- Amateur and professional league or conference executives
- College and high school administrators
- Camp and recreation club/center counselors

Table of Contents

CHAPTER

Introducing
The Code for Living

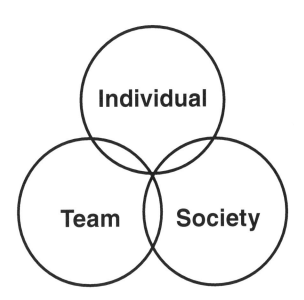

ABW's Code for Living is intended to be a unifying set of principles around which people of all ages and sports interests can join together. It is not intended to replace any of the written or unwritten codes of one's religion, family, or work, but it strives to provide unity, focus, support, and direction to those who participate in sports.

THE CODE FOR LIVING
LIFE LESSONS LEARNED THROUGH SPORTS

Because I am a role model and have the opportunity and responsibility to make a difference in the lives of others, I commit to this Code. I will take responsibility and appropriate actions when I fail to live up to it.

AS AN INDIVIDUAL:

- I will develop my skills to the best of my ability and give my best effort in practice and competition.
- I will compete within the spirit and letter of the rules of my sport.
- I will respect the dignity of every human being, and will not be abusive or dehumanizing of another either as an athlete or as a fan.

AS A MEMBER OF A TEAM:

- I will place team goals ahead of personal goals.
- I will be a positive influence on the relationships on the team.
- I will follow the team rules established by the coach.

AS A MEMBER OF SOCIETY:

- I will display caring and honorable behavior off the field and be a positive influence in my community and world.
- I will give of my time, skills, and money as I am able for the betterment of my community and world.

THE THREE SECTIONS

The Code has three sections outlining how we will behave as individuals, as members of a team, and as members of society. Just as the Pledge of

Allegiance unites Americans in a common bond, whenever a group of people share the same code, it provides the basis for a common vision and purpose. It also provides a basis for knowing what we can expect from each other. Thus, The Code becomes the basis for trust and for group solidarity.

AS AN INDIVIDUAL

- The Code provides a standard against which each of us can measure ourselves. When we review the tenets of The Code, we can determine the areas we need to improve and then develop personalized strategies for improvement. The values that stand behind The Code for Living are values on which we can all improve—all our lives. At one point in our lives we may need to work on having better discipline in our work habits. At another time, we may want to work on our relationships with others. At still another time, we may want to make greater contributions to our communities. While The Code provides a clear framework, we have the freedom to focus on different elements within it according to our ages, gifts, and circumstances. Therefore, how we choose to live it out will be a challenge that will require constant reflection, with new goals set for ourselves as each year passes.

AS A MEMBER OF A TEAM

- The Code is important for us as teammates. We are all on more than one team all the time: the family team, the work team, the neighborhood team, the school team, and even the national team because as citizens of this country we are all on the same team.
- The Code provides a common set of values on which the team can build and grow. Teams are made up of individuals, and yet a team only emerges when the individuals come together in support of common goals. The Code provides the foundation stones on which a true team can be built. The Code recognizes that we have a collective responsibility for one another and for our teams. We need each other and can only be successful with each other. In other words, no one

person can make a team. The Code represents a commitment to the team itself. When we share The Code, each person knows what he or she can expect from the other. That knowledge builds confidence and promotes team spirit.

AS A MEMBER OF SOCIETY

- The Code is important because it acknowledges the responsibility we all have as members of society, and it represents a commitment to the betterment of our communities and world. The Code makes it clear what our values are and challenges others to follow suit. It is always important for people who share common values to stand together, and by doing so, to provide an example for others to emulate.

IN THE FOLLOWING CHAPTERS

Throughout the book, you will see reference to the "playbook" as a stopping point for personal reflection or discussion. You are asked to keep a playbook (personal diary) in any form you choose (paper notebook, computer file, etc.) and to then determine the "next steps." This is truly where the work of The Code for Living begins. Meditating upon the questions or topics is the first step toward making real behavior change. These journal entries will become the foundation upon which you will build your character. Play with them. Rewrite them. Reread them. Reconsider them. Your positive momentum will fuel your motivation to continue to the next tenet in The Code for Living.

CHAPTER

Living The Code as an Individual

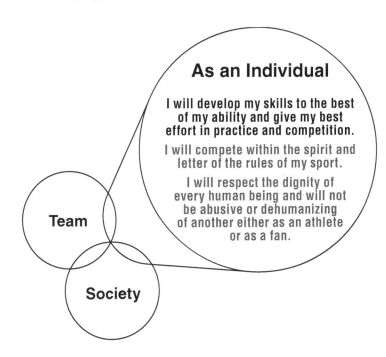

As an Individual

I will develop my skills to the best of my ability and give my best effort in practice and competition.

I will compete within the spirit and letter of the rules of my sport.

I will respect the dignity of every human being and will not be abusive or dehumanizing of another either as an athlete or as a fan.

Team

Society

THE FIRST TENET

In Chapter 2, we will break down the two elements of this tenet and discuss how they comprise the foundation for The Code for Living.

The chapter is organized this way:

"I will develop my skills to the best of my ability…"
2.1 Knowing and Accepting Your Skills and Limitations
2.2 Short-term and Long-term Goals
    Setting Goals Is Linked to Our Self-image
    Setting Goals Is Part of Our Responsibility as Teammates
    Setting Goals Is a Reflection on Those We Represent
    How to Set and Achieve Our Goals
    The Secret to Success: ABW's "Rule of Threes"
    The Big "Mo"

"… and give my best effort in practice and competition."
2.3 Work Ethic
2.4 Self-discipline

"I WILL DEVELOP MY SKILLS TO THE BEST OF MY ABILITY..."

2.1 KNOWING AND ACCEPTING YOUR SKILLS AND LIMITATIONS

In "I will develop my skills...," the key word is "my." Each of us has been given our own set of gifts and talents. Who of us has not wished that we were smarter, better looking, faster, quicker, funnier, taller, shorter, more musical, or more skilled in 1,000 different ways than we are? The first challenge we all face is to accept the skill set we have, to embrace it, and to be enthusiastic in our desire to take those skills and develop them to the best of our ability.

We are the ones who decide what is "the best of my ability." We may be able to fool others, but we should not be able to fool ourselves. We know what kind of effort we have made, and we know what kind of effort we have not made. As John Wooden observed, "Success is peace of mind, which is a direct result of self-satisfaction in knowing you did your best to become the best you are capable of becoming."

PLAYBOOK EXERCISE

- Do you agree that you should only participate in those things at which you are able to excel? Why or why not?
- What are the skills you have that you most value?
- What is the difference between doing your best and being the best?
- Do you agree with Wooden's definition of success? Why or why not?

NEXT STEPS

- Assess those areas in which you are not gifted but that you enjoy.
- What does success in those areas look like?
- What steps do you need to take to reach success in those areas?

2.2 SHORT-TERM AND LONG-TERM GOALS

We all know of the instant gratification that defines much of our world today. We want it and we want it now! But nothing that is really valuable can be achieved in an instant. It is always the result of sustained effort over a long period of time, often with serious setbacks along the way. Many of us set unrealistic goals for ourselves and then are tempted to quit when we can't achieve them. The most important rule for continued success is to set easily achievable intermediate goals for ourselves so that we have a sense of success every day.

SETTING GOALS IS LINKED TO OUR SELF-IMAGE

One of the reasons that we set goals for ourselves is out of personal pride. We may set daily goals, weekly goals, monthly goals, or seasonal goals. Whenever we set a goal, it should be something that challenges us but at the same time is achievable. When we work hard at anything, we have the satisfaction of what we have done, whether it is raking a yard, writing a paper, or learning to dribble. Our personal pride is not a reflection of how good our work is compared with that of others (the paper may not be the best in the class, we may not be the best dribbler on the team), but it's a reflection of the progress and effort we have made. It is vitally important to our own senses of self that each of us not settle for the lackadaisical. When we do that, we cannot hold our heads up, because we know we have betrayed ourselves by not giving our best effort.

SETTING GOALS IS PART OF OUR RESPONSIBILITY AS TEAMMATES

Another reason we set goals for ourselves is out of respect for our team. When we join a team, we are making a commitment to our teammates. This is not necessarily acknowledged, but it should be understood. This is why it is important for everyone to be on time for practice, to encourage one another, and to take responsibility for our time with the team. The team commits to doing its best to win. In order for the team to reach its full potential, each member must work to achieve his or her full potential. If a person misses practice or shows up late, the team suffers. Equally, if a person makes little or no effort to improve, the team suffers.

SETTING GOALS IS A REFLECTION ON THOSE WE REPRESENT

We set goals for ourselves while also knowing that we will create a positive image for those we represent: our coach, our family, our team. We are judged by those who are our teammates, family, friends, and even by those we do not know who watch us as we practice and play. Our reputation, and that of those we represent, is established by the character we exhibit day in and day out, in practice and in games.

HOW TO SET AND ACHIEVE OUR GOALS

We are all familiar with setting goals. First, we establish a long-term goal. Then, we establish objectives. Then, we determine a work plan for each objective. This is easier said than done, but determination to create a detailed plan is essential to long-term success.

THE SECRET TO SUCCESS: ABW'S "RULE OF THREES"

The Rule of Threes is the concept that when we choose a goal, we try to have three objectives, three action items for each objective, and three bite-size pieces for each action item. Now, it is hard to create that much detail some-times, but the more detail we create, the easier it is to follow our "game plan."

THE BIG "MO"

We all know about the big "Mo" (momentum) and that's what success is built on, one small success after another. The secret is to create enough small successes so that every day we are accomplishing at least one thing. It's like going on a diet—if we've lost some weight every time we get on the scale, we'll keep on trying. Similarly, if we have met achievable tasks each day, we will want to keep on succeeding.

The key to success is the positive energy that you generate by breaking your goal down into smaller steps, because the only way anyone ever gets anywhere is one step at a time. The secret is in the energy that comes from doing those bite-size pieces.

Here's what it might look like if we wanted to base creating a goal on one of the tenets:

Goal: I will be a positive influence on the other relationships on the team.

Objective 1: Overcome personal issues between two players.

Action item 1: Choose two players who have personal issues between them.

Bite-size pieces:

- Get to know each player individually.
- Invite both of them to do something with you socially.
- Find another teammate to do the same things.

Action item 2: Choose a social event just for the team: bowling, movie, party.

Bite-size pieces:

- Determine the time and place.
- Make sure everyone is coming.
- Create some funny prizes.

Action item 3: Be positive in practices.

Bite-size pieces:

- Be verbally encouraging and supportive.
- Ask others for opinions and advice.
- Be early, eager, and stay late whenever possible.

Objective 2: Get to know as many of my teammates as possible.

Action item 1: Get together with teammates individually.

Bite-size pieces:

- Choose those you know least first.
- Ask about their backgrounds, interests, etc.
- Share some personal things about yourself.

Action item 2: Be proactive outside of practice.

Bite-size pieces:

- Use locker-room time to talk to others.
- Make an effort to speak to others in class, hall, etc.
- Look for reasons to make a follow-up phone call.

Action item 3: Generate a team service project.

Bite-size pieces:

- Talk to others about ideas; solicit suggestions.
- Encourage others to take leadership.
- Celebrate afterward and compliment all.

Objective 3: This might be to repeat Objective 1 with a different two players, or you might wish to stop with only two objectives.

PLAYBOOK EXERCISE

- When was the last time you set goals for yourself?
- What is the difference between goal setting and a "to-do list?"

- Would you be willing to set goals with a peer and review them regularly?
- Do you have a sense of pride because you are moving in a clear direction?

NEXT STEPS

- Goals: Choose a goal that is achievable within thirty to sixty days.
- Prioritize: Determine how much time you will spend each day working toward that goal. Make sure it is a number you can achieve. It's better to commit to thirty minutes a day and succeed than to commit to sixty minutes and only do forty-five. You will find energy in succeeding and lose energy in failing.
- Objectives: Choose your three objectives.
- Bite-size pieces: Make sure they are easily achievable.

"... AND GIVE MY BEST EFFORT IN PRACTICE AND COMPETITION."

2.3 WORK ETHIC

Each of us must develop personal pride and respect for ourselves so that we will not cheat ourselves by giving only a half effort, by being satisfied with the sloppy, the inadequate, or anything less than our best.

But how do we do that? How do we make ourselves do the things we do not want to do? The determination to give our best effort requires tremendous self-discipline. It is always easy to quit after we have made a solid effort in practice and have become tired, or we tried hard for three-fourths of a game and now find our team well behind. The will to persevere is not different from any other skill. It requires intentional behavior: to give our best effort no matter what. And that decision must be chosen and repeated every day so it becomes a habit.

PLAYBOOK EXERCISE

- How would others describe your work ethic?
- How would you describe your own sense of pride in your efforts?

NEXT STEP

- Determine one way that you will spend five extra minutes each day after you think you are finished.

2.4 SELF-DISCIPLINE

> Nothing will work unless you do.
> — John Wooden

Each of us has known a person who worked harder than others. Each of us has seen how those who make that extra effort discover the extra dividend. Each of us has, at one time or another, taken a few more minutes each day to make something better than it would have been otherwise.

Practice requires self-discipline. Most athletes do not enjoy the drudgery of repeating the same aspect of their sport. Golfers do not want to practice the same three-foot putt for hours on end; basketball players do not want to practice the same shot over and over again, and few enjoy the rigors of conditioning. Self-discipline, grounded in the desire to excel to the best of our ability, leads us to continue to do what is best for our development, not what is most fun. The hardest part of growing up is learning that we have to do some things we do not want to do. The degree to which we are successful in that effort is usually the degree to which we are successful in whatever we are undertaking.

Many people have trouble asking for the advice and help of others. But one of the surest ways to improve is by asking others—a coach, boss, teammates, or peers—the ways they feel we could improve. We all know that it takes a big person to ask for help, but part of becoming a better person is by being a bigger person.

PLAYBOOK EXERCISE

- List the areas in which you are well-disciplined.
- List the areas in which you are less well-disciplined.
- What are some positive examples of when you have been most determined to succeed?
- When have you failed? Why?

NEXT STEPS

- Set as a goal either to be more disciplined or to strengthen your will to excel.
- Determine your objectives, action items, and bite-size pieces to succeed in your goal.

CHAPTER

Living The Code as an Individual

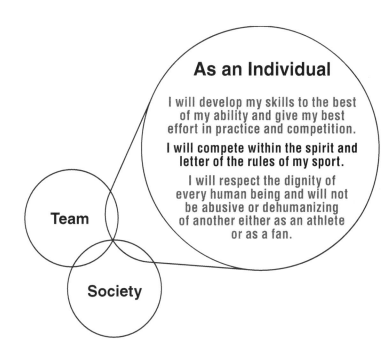

As an Individual

I will develop my skills to the best of my ability and give my best effort in practice and competition.

I will compete within the spirit and letter of the rules of my sport.

I will respect the dignity of every human being and will not be abusive or dehumanizing of another either as an athlete or as a fan.

Team

Society

THE SECOND TENET

In Chapter 3, we will examine the place of rules in our lives and in sports, and then break down the two elements of this tenet, "the spirit" and "the letter," and discuss how they are at the foundation of our lives.

The chapter is organized this way:

"I will compete within…the rules of my sport."
3.1 Thinking About Rules
3.2 Rules: The Heart of Every Game

"I will compete within…the letter of the rules…"
3.3 Truth and Honesty

"I will compete within the spirit…of the rules…"
3.4 Integrity and Honor
3.5 Courage

"I WILL COMPETE WITHIN...THE RULES OF MY SPORT."

3.1 THINKING ABOUT RULES

There is something about the word "rules" that conjures up negative feelings within us. This is because rules limit our freedom. If there were no rules, we could do anything we wanted, anytime we wanted to do it.

As children, we long to grow up because then there won't be any grown-ups to tell us what to do. We'll be free! And yet, as we grow up, we learn that rules are necessary for every aspect of life, because they provide order and structure to things. Without rules (such as laws), life would be chaotic.

PLAYBOOK EXERCISE

- What feelings (not thoughts) do you have when you hear the word "rules?"
- What thoughts do you have?
- Do you know any rules that seem to serve no purpose?

NEXT STEPS

- Determine the place of rules in your life.
- Write down the two or three most valuable personal rules by which you live. What is their purpose?

3.2 RULES: THE HEART OF EVERY GAME

A baseball umpire was once asked about the challenge and difficulty of calling pitches that were right on the line between being balls or strikes. How did he do it? "Well," he said, "there are balls and there are strikes, but they're nothing until I call them!" With baseball pitches, it is the umpire who interprets the rules of play.

It is important to acknowledge the positive value that rules provide, because they are often viewed as a necessary evil rather than the heart of the game. The truth is that it is the rules that make every game possible, as well as every great play or point in the game. Rules limit what we can do and thus provide the challenge to win a point or a game despite the difficulties thereby imposed. In other words, it is the rules of any game that not only define the game but constitute the heart and soul of the game, and so to attack the rules is to attack the game itself. Equally, the more we seek to honor and live by the rules, the more respect and honor we demonstrate for the game itself.

You may not think of it at the outset, but the way we approach the rules of a game is a direct reflection of ourselves, of the values and principles we hold. When we talk about "playing by the rules" we are not really talking about an incident here or there; we are talking about who we are at our core. Are we truthful and honorable, or are we something less than that? Do we respect the game itself above all else, or do we see ourselves as more important, with how we perform and whether we win as more important than the integrity of the game itself?

PLAYBOOK EXERCISE

- Why do you think that the rules of a sport could be thought of as being its soul?
- How does breaking the rules diminish the game itself?
- Who are the people you know who break the rules regularly?

NEXT STEPS

- Think about the love you have for your sport.
- Write down the main thoughts you have about why you love your sport.
- Determine one or more ways you can reflect that love through respect for your sport's rules.

"I WILL COMPETE WITHIN THE … LETTER OF THE RULES…"

3.3 TRUTH AND HONESTY

The way we follow the rules expresses a direct reflection of ourselves, just as the branches and the fruit of a tree reflect the health of the tree. A tree cannot produce fruit if it is unhealthy or rotten in its core. So it is with us. Telling the truth, playing with honesty and integrity is the sap that feeds our inner being. Living the truth is the fruit that others see.

This is why it is important to develop our core character at every opportunity and to recognize how "who we are" is reflected in countless ways, both on and off the field. The converse is also true. When we encounter those whose fruit is bad—that is, those who seek to skirt or flaunt the rules—we form negative opinions of them. We lose respect for those (including ourselves) who do not play by the rules.

When John Wooden was coaching at UCLA and the game was clearly won, it was not uncommon for him to call a timeout, and he did it for two reasons. First, to remind his team that the other team might let their frustration get the better of them, and not to respond or retaliate in any way for things that happened on the floor. And second, to remind them not to celebrate after the game in any way that would offend the other team or their fans. Wooden knew there were always the temptations to respond to the behavior of others, and to gloat over a particularly difficult win. It required firmness and virtue to maintain the proper behavior.

PLAYBOOK EXERCISE

- When you hear "to stand for the hard right against the easy wrong," what comes to mind in your experience?

NEXT STEPS

- Determine an issue on which you have been silent and about which you would like to stand for the "hard right." Develop a strategy for how you will do that.
- What is the next step you need to take to make yourself more "clean" than you are now? How will you do it?

"I WILL COMPETE WITHIN THE SPIRIT...OF THE RULES..."

3.4 INTEGRITY AND HONOR

Like any of our athletic skills, integrity and honor are not traits that we are born with; they are pillars of our character that are nurtured and developed through rigorous practice day after day. There is the old expression, "You are what you eat." And it can also be said that you become what you practice. Manners, decency, and moral worth are not things that can be turned on like a faucet; they are habits that are ingrained through repetition.

We know the discipline required to excel in the physical fundamentals of our sport, but how many of us spend as much time developing our inner character? How often do we see an athlete in a close game "lose it" momentarily? It may come because an opponent has been playing dirty or taunting, and the victim finally snaps, costing the team because of a resulting penalty. Or, who of us has not seen a game in which a player retaliates out of frustration to an action of an opponent, only to be caught in the retaliation and receive a major penalty? It takes far more discipline and strength of character not to respond than to respond.

The way we play the game reflects our true inner character. It is not uncommon for young tennis players to call close shots "out." In golf, beginning players routinely improve the lie of their ball, contrary to the rules. What we learn as we grow older is that we cheat ourselves in cheating the game because we compromise on our own sense of self. We are not true to ourselves or to the integrity of our sport.

Who of us has not competed against a person who broke the rules often or who played "dirty?" We have little respect for such a person, and yet that person may not realize the impact his or her behavior has on others. When we realize that cheating or playing dirty reflects on us and on what others think of us, it should make us more determined to play with honor.

We also have competed against people who play cleanly, even in the face of adversity or poor sportsmanship by another. Such people routinely apologize if they unintentionally violate an opponent or make an egregious mistake.

The most important reason to play by the spirit of the rules is because it is only when one has won the contest fairly that there is any real sense of accomplishment. A hollow feeling comes from knowing that the score does not tell the truth.

Cal Ripken Jr. tells the story of an occasion when someone tried to do the "hidden ball" trick on an opponent (when a baseball player pretends to throw the ball back to the pitcher but keeps it, hoping that the base runner will step off the bag so he can tag out the duped runner). Ripken said, "My father said, 'I don't want you ever to try that trick.'" "Why not?" Ripken asked, knowing that it was a favorite of all young players. "Because there is no honor in winning that way. Win by playing by the rules and the way the game is intended to be won."

Our lives should be an outward and visible sign of our inner character. The appeal we are making is that we reflect the spirit and not just the letter of the rule. This is the highest standard.

A wonderful example of this is one of the most memorable scenes of good sportsmanship in recent years. It took place in a women's college softball game. The batter hit a home run but while rounding first base, she somehow injured her ankle so that she could not walk. The rules require that the hitter touch all the bases. Unable to stand, she was picked up by her opposing infielders and literally carried around the bases so that she could touch them, and then they returned her to her dugout. According to the letter of the law, they could have left her on the ground and the umpire would have had to call her out.

PLAYBOOK EXERCISE

- How often do you think you are "true" to your best self? How often do you play a role that you think others will like?
- Who are examples of friends whose behavior is a reflection of who they are at their core? Who seems to you always to be playing a role?
- How would you define "honor?"

NEXT STEP

- What are the ways that personal integrity could be communicated to your team?

3.5 COURAGE

Courage is not something that everyone has in equal amounts. It is, however, like all of the virtues, something that can be nurtured, grown, and developed. When we ask for help to stand for the hard right against the easy wrong, we are asking for courage.

Courage comes in many forms. It takes courage to do something for the first time. It takes courage to trust another person to do something important for you. It takes courage to speak out or to act against the popular thing, to go against the tide of public opinion. It takes courage to act in the face of danger.

Many of us are like the lion in *The Wizard of Oz*. We are nice people who wish we were more courageous. But that is the first step: to admit we wish we were more courageous. Then we have a choice. Shall we become more courageous, or shall we remain as we are?

There are many examples of times when people are less than courageous, when the effort is made to try to fit in, to get along, to not rock the boat. It is important to know that when we are not "true to our self," as Shakespeare said, something within our soul and spirit dies. This is the consequence of not having the courage of our convictions. We lose respect for ourselves, and our own sense of self is damaged.

One of the things we have been repeating is that it takes practice to become better at anything. The same is true for courage. We become more courageous by practicing taking small courageous steps. First, think of an issue about which you disagree with others but have not told them. It would take courage for you to disagree with those with whom you have pretended to agree. Then, think of how you could express your true feelings to at least one other person. If you do that, you will find that if they are your friend, they may disagree with you, but it will not change your friendship. You will find new life and energy within for having been honest with them and with yourself. Our own inner being is inspired by the positive actions we take, just as it can be damaged by our failure to be true to ourselves. More than anything, as we take the first steps in acting courageously, we find the courage to take the next step.

Playing by the rules represents far more than playing by the rules. Who we are is expressed by how we value and live out the rules—all the rules, all the time. And who we are is far more important than any game.

PLAYBOOK EXERCISE

- What are the three virtues you consider the most important?
- Which people you know do you consider "courageous?" In what ways have they shown courage that others have not?
- What is the place of fear in your life? In what areas do you let fear determine your action?

NEXT STEP

- Choose one area in which you want to find the courage that has been lacking before. Then, have the courage to talk about it with a friend. Are you able to set some achievable goals for yourself?

CHAPTER

Living The Code as an Individual

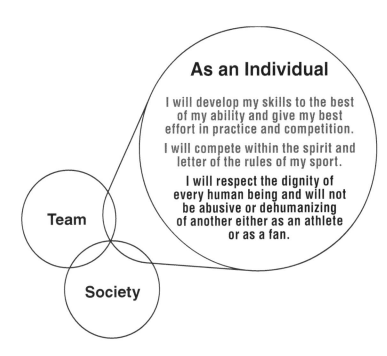

As an Individual

I will develop my skills to the best of my ability and give my best effort in practice and competition.

I will compete within the spirit and letter of the rules of my sport.

I will respect the dignity of every human being and will not be abusive or dehumanizing of another either as an athlete or as a fan.

Team

Society

THE THIRD TENET

In this chapter we will examine our attitude toward others. How do we view those who are different from us? What does it mean to "respect" others?

Are we to respect even those whose behavior is contrary to our standards? The chapter is organized in the following way:

"I will respect the dignity of every human being and will not be abusive or dehumanizing of another, either as an athlete or as a fan."

"I will respect the dignity of every human being…"
4.1 The Problem Is Not New
4.2 The Dignity of Every Person
4.3 The Barriers to Respecting Dignity
    Racism
    Religious Prejudice
    Demonizing the Opposition
4.4 Removing the Barriers
    Moments of Self-discovery and Understanding
    Moving from Tolerance to Acceptance and Inclusion

"… and will not be abusive or dehumanizing of another, either as an athlete or as a fan."
4.5 Abusive and Dehumanizing Speech
    Booing, Taunting, and Trash Talking
4.6 Developing Self-control
    Before Practice or the Game
    During the Game
    After the Game

"I WILL RESPECT THE DIGNITY OF EVERY HUMAN BEING…"

4.1 THE PROBLEM IS NOT NEW

Did you know…

…that when Jack Johnson became the heavyweight boxing champion the white community was so upset that boxer Jim Jeffries was dubbed "the Great White Hope?"

…about the negative reaction from some when Sandy Koufax of the Los Angeles Dodgers and Hank Greenberg of the Detroit Tigers refused to play in a World Series game because each game fell on Yom Kippur, the holiest day in the Jewish calendar?

…about the similar reactions when English runner Eric Liddell refused to race in the Olympics because it fell on Sunday?

…that Hitler wanted to use the 1936 Olympics in Berlin as an opportunity to showcase Aryan superiority—until the African-American Jesse Owens won four gold medals?

…that as a coach in Indiana John Wooden refused to let his team compete against a team that had previously refused to compete against another team with African-Americans on it?

The issues of race and racism, of prejudice and intolerance, have all found their challenges expressed in the world of sports. So too have sports been one of the vehicles for human growth and progress. Sports have played a major role in the transformation of individuals and society.

4.2 THE DIGNITY OF EVERY PERSON

In one sense, we have no control over our judgments and forethoughts; they simply come to us. But as thinking people we are able to rise above our immediate non-thinking reactions with a mature, reasoned response.

No matter who we are, we are likely to assume that people who look like us, dress like us, and talk like us are like us. We are usually comfortable with those who seem to be like us; however, those who are different may register different feelings within us.

What do we mean when we say we will respect the dignity of every human being? The word "dignity" is the key. It comes from the Latin word *dignus*, which means "worth." Each person has worth. Every person has value.

When the founders wrote that all men are created equal, they did not mean that all people have equal brains, looks, athletic abilities, or anything like that. They meant simply and profoundly, as Albert Schweitzer said, that "the other person is a person, just as I am." We all have the same inherent worth. No one is more of a person than anyone else.

PLAYBOOK EXERCISE

- When you see a person you don't know, what are some of the assumptions you make? Where do those stereotypes come from?
- What do "dignity" and "worth" mean to you for a person who dresses differently, speaks a different language, or comes from a different country?
- Are there some people you don't like? Do you see yourself as in some sense better than they are? What would they say about you?
- In what ways can someone say that there is a dignity or worth to every human being, no matter how badly they may behave?
- How can you show respect for a person whose behavior you find reprehensible?
- How do we learn from those who differ most from us?

NEXT STEPS

- What are the ways you can show respect for a person whose values you reject?

- Identify at least one individual or group that you think is unfairly judged by others.
- Determine at least one way you are now going to act differently toward another person. What steps do you have to take to see the other person as having worth?

4.3 THE BARRIERS TO RESPECTING DIGNITY

RACISM

RELIGIOUS PREJUDICE

DEMONIZING THE OPPOSITION

PLAYBOOK EXERCISE

- What are the attitudes you have for those people who are different from you?
- How would you describe the barriers you face in your relationships with others?
- How would you describe your views of those whose religious beliefs are different from yours?
- In what ways do you tend to pre-judge others by their race, religion, or ethnic group?
- Make a list of people you know who are of a different race, religion, or nationality from you. Does knowing these people affect your opinions about their group?
- Why do we "demonize" others?

NEXT STEPS

- Have an open conversation with someone you know whose religion or national origin is different from yours. Ask them how they understand their faith, or why it makes sense to them.
- Do the same with someone from another country. Learn what they value about their homeland and what values they appreciate most here.

4.4 REMOVING THE BARRIERS: SEEING THE OTHER PERSON AS MYSELF

MOMENTS OF SELF-DISCOVERY AND UNDERSTANDING

When Jackie Robinson broke the color barrier in baseball with the Brooklyn Dodgers in 1947, many players opposed the action. Team captain Pee Wee Reese was even presented with a petition that threatened a boycott if Robinson joined the team, but Reese refused to sign it. Then, as Robinson was being heckled by fans in Cincinnati during the Dodgers' first road trip, Reese put his arm around Robinson's shoulder in a gesture of inclusion and support.

Reese was an eight-time all-star who played with seven pennant winners and one World Series champion in Brooklyn. Carl Erskine, a pitcher on the team, also remembered Reese's role in helping Robinson break the color line in baseball. "Think of the guts that took," he said. "Pee Wee had to go home [to segregated Louisville] and answer to his friends ... I told Jackie later that [Reese's gesture] helped my race more than his."

Joe Black, a former Brooklyn pitcher and one of the first African-Americans in Major League Baseball, said, "Pee Wee helped make my boyhood dream come true to play in the majors, the World Series. When Pee Wee reached out to Jackie, all of us in the Negro League smiled and said it was the first time that a white guy had accepted us." He continued, "When I finally got up to Brooklyn, I went to Pee Wee and said, 'Black people love you. When you touched Jackie, you touched all of us.' With Pee Wee, it was No. 1 on his uniform and No. 1 in our hearts."

PLAYBOOK EXERCISE

- As a child, how did you view people of other races, religions, social and economic backgrounds?
- Think of a person you like now but did not like at first. What was the cause for the change?
- List at least two ways your views in social issues have changed. What was it that led you to change your views?
- Have you ever stood up for someone that others were making fun of as Pee Wee Reese did?

NEXT STEP

- Identify a situation in which you can make a difference by including someone who may have been left out, and work out a strategy for so doing.

MOVING FROM TOLERANCE TO ACCEPTANCE TO INCLUSION

In 1970, when Bear Bryant's University of Alabama football team was crushed 42–21 in Birmingham by the University of Southern California with African-American star Sam "Bam" Cunningham scoring three touchdowns, the stage was set for integration of the team. What Alabama fans didn't yet know was that Bryant had already crossed the color line. Sitting in the stands that day was the university's first black scholarship player, Wilbur Jackson, who watched as Sam Cunningham, in Bear Bryant's words, "did more to integrate Alabama in one afternoon than Martin Luther King Jr. had in years."

Bryant's action was similar to that of Pee Wee Reese. Just as Reese was revered in Brooklyn, so the Bear was revered in Alabama. If he was willing to accept black players on his team, then his fans would become more willing to accept them in their lives. But this was just the first step: the step of tolerance, which we take on the way to respect. Tolerance is a passive word; to say that we will "tolerate" something has the connotation of "endure" or "put up with." Not that we would enjoy something, but that we would allow it to happen or to continue. We tolerate many things: traffic to football games, rainy days, or friends who talk too much.

Tolerance means accepting the right of one person to have the same opportunity as others without necessarily embracing it or understanding it. Tolerance of another is to recognize the "letter" of the law, to use the vocabulary of our earlier tenet, but not necessarily the "spirit" of the law: the acceptance that the other person's worth equals mine. Tolerance, however, leads to the next step on the way to respect: acceptance. Acceptance means that we have internally acknowledged that a situation with which we previously disagreed is legitimate, or acceptable, even though we may not like it. When we accept something as valid, we will no longer try to fight it or stop it.

Inclusion is the final step. This is when we do not simply accept something that we previously rejected, but we actively try to make it a part of our lives. It comes when we have learned that those who are different have many positive qualities that will enhance and enrich our own lives.

"...AND WILL NOT BE ABUSIVE OR DEHUMANIZING OF ANOTHER, EITHER AS AN ATHLETE OR AS A FAN."

4.5 ABUSIVE AND DEHUMANIZING SPEECH

BOOING, TAUNTING, AND TRASH TALKING

As we enter the world of sports, we boo the official who makes a call that we either don't like or we think was wrong. We taunt opposing players, hoping to upset them and get them off their game, or simply out of meanness on our part.

Trash talking, which sometimes begins as friendly banter, often ends up with language that leads to fights or worse.

Any form of language that attacks another person is a violation of The Code, because all language that attacks a person shows disrespect for that person.

The truth is, when we use inappropriate language, the reason we are doing so is to try to hurt the person. When we trash talk opponents, we are attempting to wound their inner being in a way that will lead them to lose control of themselves in some way.

4.6 DEVELOPING SELF-CONTROL

Developing self-control is as important as any part of our character development. It comes from the result of mental discipline. Gaining control of our thoughts and words comes as the result of the same sort of consistent and ongoing work and effort that are necessary to improve our physical skills.

We all know that some people have a short fuse and others seem unflappable no matter what the situation. We are all different. But we all need to work to control our emotions. Everyone knows that the mental game is in many ways as important as the physical game. How do we develop our mental game?

BEFORE PRACTICE OR THE GAME

The first step is to "get our heads straight." This means focusing on how we plan to carry ourselves, what we plan to do, what our personal goals are for ourselves. An important part of this mental preparation is thinking through how we will deal with adversity.

Adversity can mean we are not playing well; adversity can mean the team is not playing well; adversity can mean the coach reacts in a way that we weren't expecting or our teammates say or do things we were not expecting; or it can be poor sportsmanship by our opponents or their fans. How do we react to the unexpected? All of these situations are possible, and that is why it is important to have our heads on straight!

So, what do we do? We need to remind ourselves that we will "respect the dignity of every human being… and not be abusive or dehumanizing…"

We need to remind ourselves that *this is what we will do*, no matter what the occasion or what comes up.

DURING THE GAME

Anger needs no definition; it is an emotion that we all know well. It is a powerful feeling that can build up slowly or suddenly erupt. It is so strong that it has the potential to overpower our normal thoughts and behaviors.

Emotions come to us from within. We cannot stop emotion, but we can control our reaction to it. In fact, we have to learn how to control our emotions. It is called growing up.

Some people learn how to control their emotions in only a few areas of their lives. People who yell at their five-year-old's game official, who are rude to the wait staff in restaurants, or who drive recklessly because other drivers anger them are all some examples of those who still have some growing up to do. Their emotions take control of them, and they act like children.

When we receive bad calls from an official, hear taunts from opposing players or fans, it is natural to react internally. But, externally, how do we act? Do we return the taunt verbally? Do we do we respond in some physical way? Or, do we say and do nothing, ignoring the taunt?

If we have our heads on straight, then we might say to ourselves, "We knew this would happen, and we have already determined how we are going to react. We are not going to let this get to us!" Later, as it continues, we might say to ourselves, "We knew this would continue, and we know how we are going to act." Make no mistake. This is not easy. No matter what we have determined before the game, the reality is often extremely challenging. If you are playing soccer and get tripped as you are about to take a shot and no call is made by the official, it is hard to play on as if nothing happened. If you are bumped off-stride or held by the defender just as you are about to catch a football, and no call is made, it is hard to control your emotions. But, in these and all circumstances, learning to control our emotions, rather than having them control us, is essential.

Many players, managers, and coaches are well-known for the emotional tirades and on-field antics when upset by what they consider bad officiating. But there is another way to react. When Chris Evert played tennis she was often referred to as the "ice queen," because no matter what happened for good or ill, she never changed expression. We are not suggesting that we all become that stoic in our behaviors, nor that we don't express ourselves to an official when we feel we have a legitimate complaint. Learning to control our emotions does not mean that we lose them or bury them, but it does mean that we learn how to channel them in a way that is constructive.

Some people say, "don't get mad, get even." That is not the thing to do. Instead, learn to channel the anger into positive action so that we play more determined and more focused. The great surprise is that often our refusal to respond to the taunts or behavior of others frustrates them, leading them to greater mistakes. One thing is certain: When we do not respond with anger, we earn the respect of all.

AFTER THE GAME

We have all seen people who say things after a game that they regret later, things said in anger or frustration or personal disappointment. Sometimes they are said in victory. Once words are spoken, they cannot be taken back. As children we are sometimes taught to count to ten before saying anything. One of the most difficult things to learn is the discipline necessary to hold our tongues, so as not to say things we later regret. It is better to have "no comment" than the wrong comment!

PLAYBOOK EXERCISE

- In what ways have you demonized another group in your past? Are there groups you demonize now? What about the fans of those teams you often oppose; how do you view them?

NEXT STEP

- Determine how you will act and what you will say when you hear someone using abusive or dehumanizing language.

CHAPTER

Living The Code as a Member of a Team

As a Member of a Team

I will place team goals ahead of personal goals.

I will be a positive influence on the relationships on the team.

I will follow the team rules established by the coach.

Society

Individual

THE FIRST TENET

Most sports began with the desire of the individual to play the game. The initial focus is almost always on the individual and his work or her efforts to become in some sense "good." As we begin to play on teams, we have all played with people who were more interested in how they were doing than how the team was doing. This tenet of The Code encourages sacrifice and selflessness instead of selfishness and self-centeredness. It reminds the athlete that the team goal of doing its best (and hopefully winning) is the important goal, not one's own glory, and that it is through cooperation and teamwork that that goal is best accomplished. This chapter is organized as follows:

"I will place team goals ahead of personal goals."

5.1 The Next Step in Character Development
   Sacrifice
   Cooperation
   Reliability
   Team Spirit
5.2 The Challenges
   Egos and Personality Types
   Personality Conflicts
   Injuries and Bad Luck
   Coaching Strategy
5.3 Benefits of Team Play
   Playing as a Team
   The Relationships

5.1 THE NEXT STEP IN CHARACTER DEVELOPMENT

The formation of our character requires the ongoing discipline of the will to reach our higher goals. We have seen that learning to respect others requires us to learn to control the quick impulses of our nature, and to look beyond the superficial characteristics of a person to see that individual as a valued person. We have seen that the development of our skills as an athlete requires us to submit to the daily discipline of drills and exercises in order to lead us to greater proficiency. We have seen that to play the game with honor requires us to develop the mental strength to resist the temptation to cut corners or to look for cheap ways of winning. All character development requires the continual discipline of the will to achieve a higher goal.

When we reflected on the first tenet ("Developing our skills") one of the important considerations was goal setting. We remembered that we will make the most progress if we set clear and achievable goals and work toward them. Developing our skills to the best of our ability requires discipline and work. Each of us must always strive to become the best we are capable of becoming. All personal goals, however, must be placed in the context of the team goals, and the success of the team should always be each player's highest priority.

The teams that play the best together, combining the skills of the individuals in a collective whole, are the teams that win. John Wooden always said, "I'd rather have the five players who play best together than the five best players." It is challenging for any coach to best determine the strategy and the methods of having his or her team play as one. One of the joys of coaching is to be successful; to see each person fulfilling a role and becoming a building block of the team.

SACRIFICE

It is interesting that the vocabulary of "sacrifice" has entered into baseball jargon. No ideal is more central to the concept of team play than self-sacrifice. The questions in people's minds are always, What can I do that will make the team better? What can I do that will make this play more cohesive? What can I do that will encourage others to support each other? To be a team player is to think of the team first, to make the success of a team the highest priority. It is to subsume individual interests and personal goals to the larger interests of the team.

PLAYBOOK EXERCISE

- What are some examples in which you have seen players sacrifice for their team?
- List the ways in which you sacrifice for the goals of your team, your family, or others.
- What will you lose by sacrificing for others? What will you gain?

NEXT STEP

- Determine two ways you would next like to make a difference, and what sacrifices that will require of you.

COOPERATION

Teamwork is all about cooperation, and cooperation takes place at several levels. First, cooperation begins with listening. When the coach or anyone else begins to speak, we cooperate by giving him or her our undivided attention. Communication is vital to any successful program and by cooperating and listening completely and carefully valuable time is saved. Listening shows respect for the person who is speaking and indicates that we value what that person has to say. By listening intently, the goals, strategies, or techniques may be better understood, and possible issues and problems identified. For those who are absent or who do not listen carefully, it will probably mean more time will have to be taken later, to explain again what was missed the first time. The more this occurs, the more the team's progress is delayed.

Second, cooperation includes working with our teammates to internalize and apply the lessons learned. Perhaps we can do something more easily than a teammate. We cooperate by taking the time to help that person understand or practice whatever has been taught. We cooperate by coming out to practice early either to work on our skills or to help a teammate, or by staying late.

Third, we also cooperate when we offer to help out with the little things that make our team stronger. Perhaps it's a willingness to give someone a ride, to carry equipment, to work with a teammate on a particular skill, or to support a teammate who is not playing well.

PLAYBOOK EXERCISE

- How do you see cooperation demonstrated on your team? Are there any barriers to cooperation that you see?
- Identify ways your cooperation could be improved.

NEXT STEP

- Determine a strategy for improving in the areas you identify and a timetable for action.

RELIABILITY

We often hear about playing with pain as a part of sports. Some players are known to play through injuries while others have the reputation of refusing to play if they are not at 100 percent. There are clearly times when it is unwise to play with an injury if one risks exacerbating what might be a minor injury. While we would never condone playing when there is serious risk involved, the willingness to play when suffering some sort of nagging or minor injury reflects a commitment to the team and its goals that take precedence over our own. We all rely on each other to succeed, and our reliability is often tested when we are faced with injuries.

Reliability is not just seen in these dramatic ways. It is most commonly seen in the player who is always on time, if not early. It is the person who goes the extra mile, who never complains, who volunteers, who does things without being asked, whose attitude is always positive, and who supports the team off the field in every possible way.

PLAYBOOK EXERCISE

- Make a list of the three most reliable people you depend on. What are the things they have done that have impressed you?
- Make a list of the times you have felt let down by others.

NEXT STEPS

- Ask your teammates if they think you are reliable.
- Make a list of the small things you can do that will improve your reliability in the eyes of others.

TEAM SPIRIT

Building team spirit is one of the jobs that comes both with coaching and being a team leader. Developing team spirit requires more than words. Spirit comes from within individuals, and while it cannot be demanded, it can be nurtured. Leadership by the coaching staff and individual players is key to developing team spirit, and that leadership is demonstrated by action more than by words. We respond to what we see more than what we hear. Words are only effective if they have been—and continue to be—reflected by the actions of the person who is speaking.

One of the important things that we can do is learn about the off-field lives of the team members. Are they good students? What subjects are their best? What other interests do they have? What other sports do they play? Any time coaches or players can be a part of each others' lives off the field, it increases the relationships and helps build team spirit.

It is the quality of the relationships on the team that results in commitment to each other and to the spirit of the team. Whenever we can get our players talking to each other, it helps develop bonds between them. It is only when they care about each other that they will make an extra effort for the team.

PLAYBOOK EXERCISE

- Evaluate your team's spirit. What are the positive signs that you see? Who is responsible for them?
- What are the less-than-positive things you see? Who is responsible for them?

NEXT STEP

- Determine a strategy for turning the negatives into positives and a timetable for action. Will you need someone to help you?

5.2 THE CHALLENGES

Coaches face many challenges in trying to meld a number of different individuals and personalities into one team. Unfortunately, there is no one way or easy solution to these challenges. Nothing tests a person's coaching ability more than how the coach overcomes these issues that every coach and team faces.

EGOS AND PERSONALITY TYPES

In professional sports the problem of ego gets written about a great deal, and it is a common problem. But it is not restricted to professional sports. From the youngest levels of sports there are those athletes who want to score, who want to play offense but not defense, who think they know better than others the way the team should function.

Everyone's leadership style is different. Some are aggressive, others are passive; some are vocal, others are quiet; some are disciplined, others are not; some are positive, others are negative. Bringing a diverse group of individuals into a cohesive team is a challenge. The successful coach is the person who recognizes and celebrates differences, and who helps each person understand how he or she is a part of the whole.

PERSONALITY CONFLICTS

It is inevitable that there will be individuals who do not like or get along well with others, and this is a challenge that comes with every team. Not to deal with personality issues is to foreclose on the possibility of the team reaching its full potential.

PLAYBOOK EXERCISE

- Identify a few examples of when you have been an asset to team play and when you have hindered team play.
- What personality conflicts have you had to deal with in the past? How did you handle them? What would you do differently now?

NEXT STEP

- Write out a strategy for dealing with egotistical players and for dealing with a personality conflict.

INJURIES AND BAD LUCK

Few things are more demoralizing to a team than to have one of its best players injured or to lose a game as the result of a freak play. Yet, both of these things are common in sports. A twisted knee. A torn muscle. A broken bone. A Hail Mary pass. A bad bounce. A lucky shot. A once-in-a-lifetime play. All of these combine to challenge a team's willingness to continue to make their best effort.

We are to accept injuries, bad calls, fluke plays, and the whims of sport with equanimity, knowing that whether we win or lose, victory or defeat is not as important as how we got there.

The relationships we make are also not "just a game," for these are the things that really matter, these are the things that endure, and these are the things that make life meaningful and beautiful.

The successful people are those prepared for adversity, even disaster, before it happens so that when it comes—and no matter what form it takes—they are prepared as if they had expected it to happen. They are also able to see beyond the moment to the relationships that are enduring.

COACHING STRATEGY

All good athletes think they know how to win. They think they know what offense or defense should be used, or what combination of players or positions for players would work best. In other words, players often think they know as well as or better than their coach how the team should be run.

The challenge here is for the coach to communicate well with the team. The team needs to know how and why the coach has made the decisions that have been made (why a particular offense or defense has been chosen, for example). The players need to know what the coach's thinking and philosophy is, and how that translates into the team goals.

Equally, the players should have the opportunity to share privately with the coach their own ideas and thoughts, and to have the coach demonstrate the openness and willingness to take those thoughts seriously. By listening to the concerns that individuals may have, the coach shows respect for the player and shows that he or she values the players who are presenting their ideas.

This is particularly true for younger coaches and for coaches with losing teams. Coaches who have a long and successful record will usually have their methods accepted by their players. But those coaches who are new or who have had losing seasons are more apt to have their credentials questioned by those who play and those who observe. Not surprisingly, when players are able to approach a coach with ideas, have those ideas listened to honestly and respectfully, and have the rationale for decisions communicated, the players will almost invariably become more committed to the coach and the team, whether the ideas are accepted or not.

5.3 BENEFITS OF TEAM PLAY

PLAYING AS A TEAM

One of the great experiences of sports is to play as a team. When the team comes together as one, each person realizes and values the contribution of the others and knows that each is an important part of the whole. Moreover, when the team knows it won because of the coordinated effort of everyone rather than because of simply having superior athletes, it is one of the most satisfying moments in competition. Equally, when the team knows it played its best, there is a sense of satisfaction even in defeat. There is no dishonor or regret when one is beaten by a better team.

THE RELATIONSHIPS

Many of the bonds of friendship are forged on the athletic field. When we practice together, train together, play together, struggle together, win together and lose together, we learn what it is to be together, to be together as one. The commitment that we make to the others as a member of the team, reciprocated by the others, leads to life-long friendships and commitments.

PLAYBOOK EXERCISE

- What are some of the best teams you've been a part of, in terms of teamwork and unity, not wins and losses? What were some of the worst?
- What were the keys to the good teams? The worst?

NEXT STEP

- Determine one way you can improve the relationships on the team.

CHAPTER

Living The Code as a Member of a Team

As a Member of a Team

I will place team goals ahead of personal goals.

I will be a positive influence on the relationships on the team.

I will follow the team rules established by the coach.

Society

Individual

THE SECOND TENET

Team spirit is dependent on every member of the team working together, seeking to build a spirit of unity and purpose. Relationships between team members and coaches are critical if the team is to become a real "team." In this chapter we will explore the building blocks of relationships and look into the challenges and rewards of meaningful relationships with others.

Our chapter is organized as follows:

"I will be a positive influence on the relationships on the team."

6.1 Learning to Love
6.2 Communication and the Art of Listening
    Learn to Listen
    Listen for Feelings
    Active Listening
6.3 Learning to Be a Cheerleader: The Art of Encouraging
    Look for Little Things
    Speak in Front of Others as Well as in Private
    Model the Behavior You Expect from Others
6.4 Learning to Confront Others: The Art of Dealing with Conflict
    Identify the Conflict
    Determine a Time to Deal with It
    Confront the Other Person in a Non-confrontational Way
    Set Ground Rules for Discussion
    Make "I" Statements
6.5 Learning to Reconcile: The Art of Giving and Receiving Forgiveness
    Find Common Ground
    Identify, Respect, and Honor the Feelings of the Other Person
    Make Sure Each Person Can Articulate the Other's Viewpoint
    Look for a Win-Win Solution; Make the Goal Clear
6.6 Learning to Apologize: The Art of Taking Responsibility
    Learn to Accept an Apology
    Learn the Power of Forgiveness
6.7 Five Keys to Building Positive Relationships
    Trust
    Mutual Commitment

6.1 LEARNING TO LOVE

We are all trying to learn how to love. In other words, we are all trying to learn how to build meaningful relationships that will endure. How do we say "You are important" or "I disagree with you" or "You made a mistake" or "I am sorry" so that it builds the relationship in a positive direction? As we get older we learn how important this is in all the relationships in our lives—our families, our jobs, and our teams. To completely compose our characters, we all need to learn to love.

In this chapter we will explore the main principles we need to remember as we all strive to be positive influences in our relationships with others.

PLAYBOOK EXERCISE

- How would you assess your own ability to communicate with others?
- How would others assess your ability?

NEXT STEP

- Write down one or two ways you would like to improve your ability to communicate that you care to others, and a timeline for getting there.

6.2 COMMUNICATION AND THE ART OF LISTENING

All relationships begin, continue, and end with communication. Unfortunately, it is often not good communication, and poor communication can be hurtful and destructive. Even those who care about each other may end up arguing about things in ways that undermine their relationship. Good communication requires work and discipline, just like any other skill. Here are the components we need to practice:

LEARN TO LISTEN

As children we all were told, "You have two ears and one mouth; that's because it's more important to listen than to speak." There is some truth in that. But it's also true that just listening is not enough. To listen to the other person, we have to care about and value the other person. We can be "listening" without really hearing! We can tell if people are truly interested in what we have to say or if they are just letting us talk. It takes effort to listen to many people. We need to acknowledge that and determine that we will make the effort.

The difficult task of "just listening" reminds us that:
- We are not listening if we are thinking about our response while someone is still talking.
- We are not listening if we are thinking that we have already heard this before and know what we think about it.
- We are listening if we are giving the speaker our full attention.
- We are listening if we ask follow-up questions to test our understanding or to elicit more information.

LISTEN FOR FEELINGS

We all have thoughts and feelings. Our thoughts and opinions are important to us. Usually that is the level at which we speak: "I think we need to work harder." Or, "I don't think everyone gave the best effort." Thoughts are important, but feelings have more power. Great speakers generate and connect with the feelings within us. Whenever we can tap into the feelings of others, we are tapping into their hearts.

An important first step is attempting to identify the feelings of the speaker. A teammate might say, "We all have to do our best, and I don't think we did our best yesterday," but what is he or she really saying? Is it, "I'm disappointed," or "I'm mad," or "I'm really talking to just one person," or "I'm better than you," or what? In response, you could say, "I agree with you. We need to do our best." But, it would probably be better if you said, "It sounds to me like you're angry," or "disappointed," or "frustrated." That is, it would be better if you could try to identify the feeling. This would allow the speaker to say, "Yes, I am angry because…" The answer may not be as you assumed (as we will see later). It's usually more helpful to talk about feelings than thoughts.

Many men have more difficulty talking about their feelings than women do. Generally, men have traditionally been culturally raised to be tough, in-control, goal-oriented, and not given to caring about their feelings. Their feelings are to be suppressed, and the focus is always on the object or the goal, not on any "sissy" feelings they may have. It is hard for many men to express their feelings because they are not in touch with them. They may be mad but not understand why. For example, a player might blow up at a teammate because he's mad the team lost. But that mad feeling may not just be because the game was lost; it may have come from weeks earlier when that teammate missed practice or didn't take a particular technique seriously. Now, when the game is lost, all that past feeling erupts. How much better it would have been had the player identified his feelings and said, "I'm really mad because I'm frustrated, because you have goofed off in practice for weeks." How much better things could have turned out if that player had been able to express his feelings by saying something similar weeks earlier when he became upset!

Or, a player might be upset after a loss because he or she always wanted to have an undefeated season and now that goal will not be achieved. So, in this case, the player is not so much angry as sad and disappointed that he or she will not be able to hit an important goal.

So, listening for feelings involves listening for the feeling that is behind the words being spoken. It also involves listening for the feelings that are stirred up inside us, identifying them, and then trying to figure out why we have those feelings. What are the feelings that go with those reactions? Where do those feelings come from? Our own feelings often come from places we do not realize at first. When we learn how to identify what our own feelings are, we begin to learn who we are. As we learn who we are, we can work to see things differently, then we can change and grow as we are able to see areas needing improvement.

ACTIVE LISTENING

A key technique to learn is what is called "active listening." It is called "active" because rather than just allowing a person to talk, we actively check out what we think we are hearing, by testing for feeling. Here's an example:
Person one: Coach was really on us today. Made us do extra wind sprints.
Person two: Sounds like you're a little mad with the coach.
Person one: Yes, I am; we should be doing extra drills, not sprints.

In this case, we tested our assumption about the feeling ("Sounds like you're mad") and were confirmed in it.

Here's another way it could have gone:
Person one: Coach was really on us today. Made us do extra wind sprints.
Person two: Sounds like you're a little mad with the coach.
Person one: No, I'm not. I'm glad he did. We need better conditioning.

In this case, we tested our assumption about the feeling ("Sounds like you're mad") and found out we were wrong. If we do not engage in active listening, in testing our assumptions, we may misunderstand what is being said. This happens all the time, as the last example shows.

Another example:
Person one: Coach Jones doesn't know what he's doing.
Person two: Sure he does; he's won two state titles.
Person one: No, he's a moron.

Here's another way it could have gone:
Person one: Coach Jones doesn't know what he's doing.
Person two: Sounds like you're really mad at him.
Person one: I sure am. He won't let me try another position.

By listening for feelings, we learn why our teammate is mad at the coach. If we had pursued our first instinct, to defend the coach, we might not have learned why our friend was mad at the coach.

By participating actively, we are checking out the feelings of the speaker. When we respond, we need to try to respond to the feelings, not to the words themselves. We can always come back to the words, but the feelings are the key point.

PLAYBOOK EXERCISE

- Would others say that you are a good listener?
- Are you able to identify the feelings you have at any given time?
- Did you understand "active listening?" Have you ever practiced it?

NEXT STEPS

- Determine a relationship you are going to work on.
- Practice "active listening" intentionally for one day. What surprised you the most in doing it?

6.3 LEARNING TO BE A CHEERLEADER: THE ART OF ENCOURAGING

We all benefit by being encouraged in whatever we are undertaking. Tennis great Althea Gibson said that no one ever became a champion without having a key person who believed in and encouraged him or her. We all need people who believe in us and stand with us no matter how we perform on any one day. Positive energy generates positive responses from others.

To help create positive relationships on the team, each person must do his or her part to contribute to the whole. Encouraging and cheerleading must be genuine. Empty words are understood as such and create a negative experience for others. Here are some key tips to practice as we seek to be encouragers on our team:

LOOK FOR LITTLE THINGS

Maintaining positive relationships requires ongoing effort. It's important to look for the little ways we can encourage and support others. The obvious thing is to commend things that are typically taken for granted, such as a good pass or a special effort. A key in this is to actively look for ways to be positive. We can also be positive by asking about *things we can't see*. For example, a simple "How are things going for you?" asked in a way that communicates real interest may lead to an important conversation about a personal issue unrelated to sports. All the bonds of friendship that are built will ultimately strengthen the team.

SPEAK IN FRONT OF OTHERS AS WELL AS IN PRIVATE

Learning to share a kind word and to look for opportunities to encourage others is an important way to maintain and develop our friendships and relationships. While this will often happen one-on one or in the presence of one or two others, it is important to look for ways to commend others publicly, such as in front of the whole team. There are always key moments when a particular word spoken or person acknowledged can make a significant difference. Most importantly, we should always be sincere in what we say. Idle "rah-rah" chatter will be understood as insincere and should be avoided. In that way, when something is important and we want to be heard, our words will carry real weight. Remember the story of the boy who cried wolf? No one wants to be that boy!

MODEL THE BEHAVIOR YOU EXPECT FROM OTHERS

The truth is that what we do is more important than our words; our daily actions establish our credibility. The person who slacks off in practice and gives less than 100 percent in a game will have no credibility if he or she says, "Let's go, we can do it!" On the other hand, the person who has already earned the respect and admiration of teammates will be heard.

PLAYBOOK EXERCISE

- Would your friends describe you as an encourager?
- What are the ways you think you encourage others?
- What are the ways you fail to encourage others?

NEXT STEPS

- Determine a strategy for becoming more of an encourager.
- Include one way that you can model the behavior you expect from others.
- Set a date to evaluate your efforts.

6.4 LEARNING TO CONFRONT OTHERS: THE ART OF DEALING WITH CONFLICT

Conflict is inevitable when you have a group of individuals who are motivated and committed to achieving a goal as a team. This is natural because personalities are all different and because we approach things in different ways. Conflict is not necessarily a bad thing. Handled properly, it can create conversation that leads to clarity and focus for those involved—and to greater commitment as well.

It is always better to be proactive in any situation involving conflict. Things rarely, if ever, "simply go away." Feelings and emotions that are suppressed will always have a way of coming out, usually in unfortunate ways and at inopportune times.

Here are some steps to take in any situation:

IDENTIFY THE CONFLICT

Determine if there is an issue between one or more team members. Sometimes it's obvious; other times it may be something that is under the surface, unspoken, but destructive. If one person harbors feelings for another, it will reveal itself in indirect (if not direct) ways. Those negative feelings will always surface, either passive-aggressively or in the form of a team that lacks positive energy and chemistry.

DETERMINE A TIME TO DEAL WITH IT

There is a time and a place for everything. Public blowups usually result in bigger hurts and bigger problems that often could have been avoided with some forethought. In any event, conflicts are best resolved in an appropriate atmosphere.

CONFRONT THE OTHER PERSON IN A NON-CONFRONTATIONAL WAY

It is important to approach people that are having a conflict in a way that does not make them defensive or angry. In many ways, the approach may have a lot to do with how successful you are going to be. If it is handled poorly, it will only make things worse. Here are some suggested ways of approaching someone, all of which are intended to open up lines of communication:

"I have something important I want to talk about."

"I need to talk to you sometime when it's good for you."

"Could we get together some time? There's something bothering me and I'd like to talk about it."

When the other person says, "What is it?" resist the temptation to tell them! Just say, "I'd like to wait until we have time to talk about it." In other words, unless you have time to sit down for at least 30 minutes with the door shut, do not try to do it quickly just to get it over with.

SET GROUND RULES FOR THE DISCUSSION

When you do meet, start by setting the ground rules for discussion. This is particularly necessary if you have two or more people present who are having a conflict with each other.

MAKE "I" STATEMENTS

This is very important. When we make "I" statements we begin the sentence with "I," and so we only focus on ourselves and how we feel. We do not try to describe what other people are doing or saying; we only say how it affects us. Rather than saying "You always say X," it is better to say, "I get angry when I see or hear X." By only making "I" statements we are able to let everyone know how their information and viewpoints have been heard. We do not talk about what we think is going on in another person's head. We only talk about how we feel, or felt, when something happens or has happened.

No language that attacks or demeans another is permitted.

Each person gets to speak without being interrupted.

We will continue this process in the next section.

PLAYBOOK EXERCISE

- This chapter has outlined a process for beginning to deal with conflict. Do you agree with it? In what ways do you disagree?
- Analyze how you have handled conflicts in the past.
- What will your strategy be to deal with a conflict you are facing now?

NEXT STEPS

- Ask a few friends how they think you do in handling conflict. Practice your listening skills as they speak.

- What is something important that you have learned or been reminded of?

6.5 LEARNING TO RECONCILE: THE ART OF GIVING AND RECEIVING FORGIVENESS

FIND COMMON GROUND

The starting point to conflict resolution should be finding the common ground on which we stand. By this we mean that we are all on the same team, we all want to be successful, and we are all committed to that effort. It is important for each person to recognize and affirm those common desires. This section includes some ways you can help others when a conflict arises.

IDENTIFY, RESPECT, AND HONOR THE FEELINGS OF THE OTHER PERSON(S)

It is not always easy to identify the feelings or the problem. Several issues may have become layered on top of one another. The real source of the feelings of anger or hostility may or may not be easy to determine. However, it is important to work as hard as possible to articulate the feelings and actions that have brought on this conflict. All thoughts and feelings should be symbolically laid out on a table in a non-judgmental way.

MAKE SURE EACH PERSON CAN ARTICULATE THE OTHER'S VIEWPOINT

After each person has shared his or her thoughts and feelings, ask each person to repeat what the other person said. It is important that it is repeated as it was originally shared, without any comments. For example, if the second person does not articulate what the first said, then the first should repeat it until the first is satisfied that the second has understood it correctly.

LOOK FOR A WIN-WIN SOLUTION; MAKE THE GOAL CLEAR

Ask if each understands why the other is conflicted. When they have agreed that each understands the other, then the question becomes, what do we have to do to work this out? Let them know that you are looking for a win-win solution. It may be that one person needs to apologize; it may be that both need to apologize. However, apologizing does not necessarily guarantee success. The apology must be accepted by the other, and sometimes this is not easily granted. In some cases, more than an apology may be warranted.

6.6 LEARNING TO APOLOGIZE: THE ART OF TAKING RESPONSIBILITY

It is usually difficult to apologize. It means admitting that we made a mistake. But healing cannot take place in a relationship or on a team as long as something is broken. It needs to be fixed. Often, situations have gotten complicated, with more than one person responsible for the situation, and so one person does not want to apologize if that person thinks that others are being let off the hook. However, one person does not have to take the responsibility for the whole conflict, but can take responsibility for his or her part. It should be easy to say, "I am sorry for my part in all of this. What I did was wrong and so I am sorry that I did what I did, or said what I said." Even if we did not cause the conflict, if we played any part, however small, we should regret it and be willing to offer our apology.

LEARNING TO ACCEPT AN APOLOGY IS A NECESSARY STEP

When others are willing to humble themselves and admit that they made a mistake for which they are sorry, we should always be willing to forgive them. At times this is difficult to do because we may have been hurt very badly, and even an apology cannot heal a deep wound easily. However, it is good to remember that we are all imperfect, and that by apologizing, the other person is acknowledging that he or she has flaws and is asking to be forgiven.

Recognizing the truth of that may help make it easier for us to accept the apology and to know that we all share a common humanity.

LEARNING THE POWER OF FORGIVENESS TO HEAL RELATIONSHIPS

When we have been in conflict with another, when we are able to forgive and be forgiven, we discover a new life, a new energy. The act of forgiving touches both people, and indeed its power will carry over to the whole team.

PLAYBOOK EXERCISE

- Write down your thoughts on forgiveness. When was a time you were forgiven?
- Can you think of a significant time when you forgave someone?
- What were your feelings before, during, and after the discussion of forgiveness?

NEXT STEPS

- Determine a person you need to forgive and how you will do it.
- Put down a date by which you will have taken that next step.

6.7 FIVE KEYS TO BUILDING POSITIVE RELATIONSHIPS

Communication is the key to all relationships, and the challenge of learning to communicate in a clear and effective way cannot be overstated. There are five additional keys to test ourselves against and to work to improve on all the time. We have touched on some of these points in previous chapters, but it is good to remember them in this context.

TRUST

We, teammates and coaches, must be able to trust each other. Trust means that we will be honest with each other, that we will do the things we commit to doing, and that we will never betray or undermine the other in any way. This is tough because players and coaches like to talk to each other about others; it is easy to want to make ourselves look better by saying something negative about someone else.

MUTUAL COMMITMENT

Commit to each other and to the goals of the team. To have positive relationships on the team, everyone must be committed to the team goals. If it is clear that someone is not committed in this way, or has other conflicts, this must be dealt with by everyone.

WILLINGNESS TO SACRIFICE

On the other side of the commitment coin, our commitment to each other and to the well-being of the team is measured by our willingness to do all we can to help our team succeed.

CONTINUAL WORK

Developing relationships takes continual work. Like any skill, relationship building must be practiced daily, refined and developed. New skills and techniques can always be learned. There are many days when we don't feel like practicing, but as in any skill development, those are the days we have to will ourselves to continue.

HONEST COMMUNICATION

Communication is the key, as we have said. But it can be misused as well. To be a positive influence, we must always resist the temptation to manipulate others. Few things are more tempting than trying to manipulate someone into doing something or believing something. People who manipulate one person usually will do it to others as well, and those affected will eventually realize that they were not being dealt with honestly. Then trust and the relationship are damaged, if not destroyed.

PLAYBOOK EXERCISE

- Are you a person others can trust? What evidence do you have for or against your response?
- Do you think everyone is willing to make the same commitment to the team? Can you measure it?
- Do you think you are honest and straightforward in your dealings with others? What would they say? Why?

NEXT STEPS

- Determine a relationship you would like to work on.
- Develop a plan for several different ways you can work on this relationship in the coming weeks. Try to put down clear and measurable objectives so that you can judge how you have done.

6.8 PRACTICAL ISSUES

A number of practical issues relate to maintaining positive relationships on the team. It is important to consider them separately.

OUR OWN NEEDS AND WANTS

No matter who we are, we need to know what it is that we want and expect out of others; we also must know what we will get from them. If we have expectations that others are not aware of, our relationships will soon sour. We have talked about this under the rules established by the coach, but it is important in every aspect of being on a team.

THE ROLE OF THE CAPTAIN

The captain has the opportunity to serve as a leader of the team. It is possible that every player can play a leadership role at various times, and many do, but it is the expectation that the captain will serve as both official and unofficial leader of the team. The captain should play a role that is natural and consistent with his or her personality rather than try to emulate some imagined role. If the captain's behavior is consistent with who he or she is, the captain should play a significant role in developing the unity, cohesiveness, and spirit of the team.

BULLYING

It should be unnecessary to bring this up. However, bullying has become such a large problem in today's schools that we wish to address it. Coaches should make it clear to their teams that no form of bullying, teasing, or abuse of any member of the team by anyone at any time in any place will be tolerated. Further, given the situation in so many schools, the expectation should be that all players will be proactive in sticking up and standing with any teammate (or anyone!) who is ever the subject of any form of bullying by anyone, no matter where it occurs.

PLAYBOOK EXERCISE

- How would you describe the relationships on your team?
- Can you identify any individual or group on your team that causes your team to be divided in any way?

NEXT STEPS

- Identify the member of your team that you dislike the most or who gives you the most trouble.
- Work out a plan for improving your relationship with this member of the team.

CHAPTER

Living The Code as a Member of a Team

As a Member of a Team

I will place team goals ahead of personal goals.

I will be a positive influence on the relationships on the team.

I will follow the team rules established by the coach.

Society

Individual

THE THIRD TENET

Order, discipline, and a coordinated effort by the entire team is the responsibility of the coach. One of the keys to the coach's leadership is the rules established by the coach. They often set the tone and the character of the team. We will explore this tenet in the following way:

"I will follow the team rules established by the coach."

7.1 Freedom and Authority
7.2 Laws and Rules
7.3 Only One Captain on the Ship
   The Coach as the Authority
7.4 Explaining the Rules
7.5 Personal Honesty: Honoring the Rules
7.6 Living into Freedom and Obedience

7.1 FREEDOM AND AUTHORITY

When we are children we all want to be free from the control of our parents. We cannot do all the things we want to be able to do, and we long for freedom. Freedom comes in the form of a driver's license for many teenagers. It's the first time they are not dependent on their parents to take them wherever they want to go. When we first do something by ourselves, we are thrilled with the new feeling of freedom that we experience.

We soon learn that there is no such thing as freedom, that while being free means we are free to choose, we must live with our choices. Freedom is a burden. We have to choose how we spend every second of our lives. It is no longer our parents telling us what we cannot do; we are choosing what we will do.

Freedom is a burden.

So, how do we make our choices? At first, we do the things we want to do, that others do, or that we were taught. It begins as an unthinking process. For some people this process can go on for a very long time. Sooner or later, however, we realize that we have to decide who we will become as a person. What are our values? What will our character look like?

The question that stands behind and within these questions is, what authority do we recognize? Authority is an important word. By it we mean, what is it that governs our lives? Are we always going to do only what is best for us? Or, are we only going to do what is best for others? When we decide, what is the basis for our decision?

What authority do we recognize?

In other words, we are asking, "What is your Code for Living?"

As we have already observed, there are many different codes for living. Religious beliefs, cultural traditions, family values, and civic duties all make up overlapping value systems through which we forge our identity by making our choices.

We all need to live under authority. This is not what we want to hear or believe. We want to be our own authority. But those who try to live alone and without authority set themselves up for their own downfall, whether as an individual, in a family, in a business, or in a career. Those who break the legal authority will be brought to justice, and those who have no moral authority often will see their lives self-destruct sooner or later.

ABW does not seek to discourage any of the personal beliefs or faith traditions of anyone. In fact, we encourage everyone to consider seriously all the sources of meaning and value that are, can, or should be a part of their lives. The purpose of The Code is to provide common ground on which we can all stand, no matter what our personal faith or value system may be. The Code, as an authority in our lives, reflects beliefs and values that we have already accepted from our own faith tradition, our parents, or other people we respect and admire. In any event, we need to build our lives under an authority (or authorities) greater than ourselves.

PLAYBOOK EXERCISE

- Make a list of the authorities you recognize in your life.
- Put down the evidence others would see for the authorities in your life.

NEXT STEPS

- Choose an authority that you would like to make a bigger part of your life.
- Determine a measurable strategy for making this happen.

7.2 LAWS AND RULES

In the United States we consider ourselves to be a free people. We have the freedom to choose our religion, to say whatever we wish, to travel and move wherever we desire, and to make our own decisions. Our freedom, however, is not limitless. The courts have determined that we can exercise our freedom as Americans only insofar as it does not interfere with another person's freedom. For example, we have speed limits on the highway to help ensure that people arrive safely at their destinations. And while we have freedom of speech, we cannot yell "fire, fire!" in a crowded theatre because that may result in a stampede that could harm others. We can travel on an airplane, but we will have to be searched first so any potentially harmful items can be discovered and confiscated.

The authority of the law provides for order and safety in society. In the military, the chain of command provides an authority for order. The boss provides for order in the workplace. The parent provides for order in the home.

7.3 ONLY ONE CAPTAIN ON THE SHIP

The coach is the authority on the team, the person who provides order. When the authority of the coach is accepted and honored, the team has its best chance for success. This does not mean that the strategies, methods, or systems that the coach employs cannot be discussed. The coach's authority is enhanced by openness to the ideas of suggestions of others. But there is a time and a place for everything.

All good coaches have rules for their team. Depending on the sport and the team, there are usually a variety of rules: training rules, practice rules, off-the-field rules, and travel rules. Some coaches will include academic rules. Some rules are obvious, such as being on time to practice. Others are less obvious. For example, when traveling, the coach might require a dress code that is more formal than normal school dress. Perhaps this is so the team can look good when they travel together, or it could be because the coach is seeking to add another layer of pride, identity, and bonding to the team.

THE COACH AS THE AUTHORITY

In joining a team, we agree to submit to the authority of the coach. At times this is easy, and at other times it can be challenging. What do we do when we disagree with the coach? The good coach, like any good leader, will make it known how and how not to raise questions. As a member of the team, each person must follow the rules established by the coach.

PLAYBOOK EXERCISE

- Write down a few examples of when you followed the directions of others with which you disagreed.
- In what ways are you a good follower? In what ways are you not a good follower?
- Do you think a chain of command is a good thing in every situation? If not, in what situations is an alternative method better?

NEXT STEP

- Determine at least one way that you can demonstrate to others your commitment to the direction of your coach.

7.4 EXPLAINING THE RULES

When John Wooden was the basketball coach at UCLA he began every year with a lesson in how to put on socks and shoes. You can imagine how the players reacted! Some were All-Americans and all of them had been putting on socks and shoes most of their lives. But Wooden was insistent on this ritual every year because he did not want any of his players to develop blisters if the socks were improperly put on. In doing this, I am sure that the players also learned the importance of details—and the kind of attention to detail that their coach expected of them. Explaining his way of putting on the socks and shoes also taught them how they were to approach every aspect of being on that team.

Nothing breeds grumbling easier than asking young people to do something they don't see any reason to do. When we have asked an authority figure why we should do something, we have all heard at one time or another, "Because I said so!" And that has at times confused or angered us. At a minimum, we need to understand why we are being asked to do things. We may disagree with the value, but at least we will understand the thinking behind the request.

Players will all understand the importance of being at practice on time and of supporting each other, but some may not understand the training rules or practices of the coach. It is important for the coach to take the time at the beginning of the year to articulate his or her philosophy as expressed through the rules (and other expectations for the team).

7.5 PERSONAL HONESTY: HONORING THE RULES

Many of the coach's rules can be easily followed, but some can be easily broken. There is an old saying, "Discipline is what you do when no one is watching." No one knows if you break a training rule by having an alcoholic drink in your room or staying up too late. But you know. What you have is more than a rules violation; it is a failure to do your duty, to live up to what is possible and best in you. It is your failure to live up to your commitment to the team.

Failure in the small things is as important as failure in the big things. We do not naturally see things that way all the time. We want to believe that our character is determined based on the truly important things. But it is more likely that the opposite is true. The person who honors the smallest commitment, who attends to the smallest detail, who seeks to do his or her best in the small things will more likely be consistent with the large things. The one who slacks off in small things is not as disciplined and as conditioned to carry through on the big things. If we can win the small battles and succeed in the daily challenges, then we will forge a character that is solid from the bottom up.

PLAYBOOK EXERCISE

- Do you and your team understand the reason for your rules?
- Are there any rules that cause difficulty for others?
- How do the spirit and the letter of the rules differ?

NEXT STEP

- Determine at least two ways you can better honor the rules in your situation.

7.6 LIVING INTO FREEDOM AND OBEDIENCE

The irony of having an authority over us is that it frees us as it limits us. When we choose the direction for our life, the authority we must recognize will become clear. When we submit to that authority, it will provide the blueprint on which we can then build a successful life. The Code for Living reminds us that we are going to do our best, we are going to respect others, we are going to play by the rules, and we are going to put team goals ahead of our personal goals. These are all the markers on the path to a fulfilled life, a life with meaning and purpose.

CHAPTER

Living The Code as a Member of Society

As a Member of Society

I will display caring and honerable behavior off the field and be a positive influence in my community and world.

I will give my time, skills, and money as I am able for the betterment of the community and world.

Individual

Team

THE FIRST TENET

We come now to the final section of The Code, which outlines our responsibility as citizens of our country and members of society. Some of the values

WINNING MORE THAN THE GAME

that have already been articulated will reappear in this section, but this is to be expected for a simple reason: We should live lives of consistency. In other words, the values that determine how we will act as individuals, or as members of a team, will inevitably also come into play as we reflect on our role off the field and in the community.

This chapter is organized this way:

"I will display caring and honorable behavior off the field and be a positive influence in my community and world."

8.1 When You Know Who You Are, You Know How to Act
8.2 Excellence Should Always Be the Standard
8.3 Displaying Caring and Honorable Behavior
8.4 Being a Positive Influence

8.1 WHEN YOU KNOW WHO YOU ARE, YOU KNOW HOW TO ACT

The primary purpose of this book has been to help us compose our character, to forge who we are, to determine the values that are important to us and to live them out by making them visible to others. It's true: When we know who we are, we will know how to act. It's also true that "growing up" or "forming our character" is something that begins when we are young but is never fully completed. Hopefully, we will continue to grow and mature throughout our lives.

When we go through our adolescent years we are particularly focused on discovering our individuality. Who are we? How are we going to act? We try out different clothes, haircuts, types of music and so on. Do we wear the same kind of clothes that everyone else does, or the ones we like? Do we try to act like others? Or do we try to think things through, and try to choose our own way? Everyone wants to be unique, but everyone also wants to have friends. If we are "different," we are afraid we may not fit in, and so there is great pressure to conform.

PLAYBOOK EXERCISE

- When have you have tried to conform to what your friends were doing?
- When do you go against the crowd?
- What is the greatest peer pressure you face?
- Do you think your behavior reflects your values? What would others say?

NEXT STEPS

- What part of your identity would you like to work on next?
- Make a list of ways you can grow in that area.

8.2 EXCELLENCE SHOULD ALWAYS BE THE STANDARD

All athletes train for hours each day to become skilled at their sport, and excelling off the field of play also requires training. For the high-profile athlete, learning how to respond to a reporter, a young admirer, or a crowd at a charity event is a skill that can be developed, and it takes the same effort and patience as developing any other skill. The same is true for all of us. We all have to take our presence and influence in the world as seriously as we take our family life or professional life.

There is an old saying "It's better to tell the truth, because then you don't have to remember what story you said to anyone." The same is true for our behavior. If we act in a way that is consistent with who we are, then all we have to do is act naturally. On the other hand, if we like to have loose lips in some situations but not in others, then we have to always be thinking about how we are going to behave: Will it be the loose-lips person or the well-mannered person? Obviously, if we play different roles according to where we are, we're not true to ourselves.

Coach John Wooden said, "It's more important to have character than to be a character." There is always a temptation to be cute, outrageous, or controversial. Again, it is tempting to act in ways that may not reflect the person we want to be. We have all said the wrong thing at one time or another, something that did not reflect the way we wanted people to think of us!

> It's more important to have character than to be a character.
> — John Wooden

Our reputation is a reflection of our character. Living up to our best selves is the standard of excellence to which we should all naturally aspire. There can be no goal higher than to be held in the high respect and admiration of others. A person's reputation is his or her most valuable asset, and what can take years to establish can be lost in one foolish decision.

As we have observed throughout this book, our attitude more than anything determines how far we go toward achieving our goals. Henry Ford said, "Whether you think you can or you can't, you're right." We all have different skills and abilities, but it is our attitude that determines our work ethic, and our resolve pushes us to do whatever is necessary to achieve our goals.

PLAYBOOK EXERCISE

- Do you think you treat all people the same? Would others agree with your answer?
- Can you name one or more people who treat everyone the same? How can you tell?
- What do you think other people say when your name is spoken?
- Who is a person whose behavior you most admire? What is one of his or her character traits you would like to have?

NEXT STEP

- Make a calendar of how you spend your time for one week, and if it didn't end up the way you wanted, make changes for the next week.

8.3 DISPLAYING CARING AND HONORABLE BEHAVIOR

When we think about our role in our community and world, how would we describe it? Are we active, involved, and committed, or are we passive, uninspired, and disinterested? The Code uses the word "display" to describe the expectation to which we are committing. "Display" means to show, exhibit, or reveal. While this can include private or anonymous acts, it has as its primary meaning something that is done publicly, of which one or more people are aware. So, we are not to be silent, unaffected observers of what is going on, but rather people who visibly demonstrate caring and honorable behavior.

Honorable behavior does not mean that we are to automatically assume a certain position on any subject—or that there is always a right and a wrong view on any subject. It does mean, however, that whatever we say or do will merit the respect of others for the way we speak and conduct ourselves.

Equally, however, we should not assume that to display a certain behavior necessarily assumes that we are vocal leaders. Rather it means that in our public life, we will always conduct ourselves in a way that is viewed as positive, respectful, and understood by all. There may be times when displaying caring and honorable behavior will, nevertheless, serve to make others angry. The most important lesson to be learned is how to disagree without becoming personal. We must always resist the temptation to enter into the culture of gossip, innuendo, and personal attacks on individuals that has become popular on television, on radio talk shows, in politics, and in virtually every aspect of society.

The easiest way to go through life is to go with the flow. This means agreeing with the opinions of others without reflection, and conforming with whatever the majority thinks or believes about anything. There are certainly many times when we may not be interested in issues or problems, but the temptation to "get along by going along" does not challenge us as individuals to become our best selves.

To display caring and honorable behavior can be one thing when we are speaking to sympathetic ears, but it can be a difficult thing when we are in the minority of what we are supporting. Those are the occasions when it requires courage to be true to ourselves.

PLAYBOOK EXERCISE

- When is a time that you tend to go with the flow, when you wish you were more assertive?
- What is one area in which you have displayed honorable and caring behavior?

NEXT STEP

- Each day for the next week, look for an occasion when you can deliberately demonstrate caring and honorable behavior.

8.4 BEING A POSITIVE INFLUENCE

In all of our lives there are people we are always glad to see. They are a positive influence in our lives because we know they value us and have our best interests at heart. Whether they are family members, friends, or professional associates, they have a caring nature and genuine concern for us that enriches our lives.

What are the characteristics of these people?

First, they are positive, always looking for and expecting the best in others and in any situation. There is an unmistakable positive energy around them that is revealed in their demeanor and reflected in their words and actions.

Second, they are good listeners. They're more interested in us and what we have been doing (and are doing) than in their own lives. They are more likely to speak last than first. They always let you know that they value you and what you have to say.

Third, they are more apt to ask questions than give answers. They will be as enthusiastic for the ideas of others as for their own. In fact, they are more interested in finding the best solution to any issue than in having their own way.

Fourth, they take advantage of every opportunity to make even the smallest difference. They touch what needs to be loved, help heal whatever is broken, and make us more alive by being a part of our lives.

Fifth, they are always considerate and kind. Thoughtfulness and consideration for others are the bedrock of good manners.

PLAYBOOK EXERCISE

- Name three people who have good manners. How can you tell?
- Compare your life with the five characteristics listed at the end of this section. How do you stack up?

NEXT STEPS

- Pick one of the five characteristics and work on displaying it intentionally for a week.

CHAPTER

Living The Code as a Member of Society

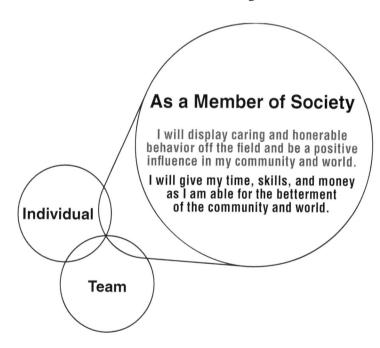

As a Member of Society

I will display caring and honerable behavior off the field and be a positive influence in my community and world.

I will give my time, skills, and money as I am able for the betterment of the community and world.

Individual

Team

THE SECOND TENET

By now it has become clear that the composing of our character has to include an awareness of and a participation in the community and world in which we live. Community service is not a value that everyone automatically assumes or shares. We will make no assumptions as we explore this tenet in the following way:

"I will give of my time, skills, and money as I am able for the betterment of my community and world."

9.1 From Passive Indifference to Active Participation
    To Become a Giver
    Members of the Human Family
    Finding Meaning
    The Meaning of Citizenship
9.2 Discovering the Power of Giving
    Compassion Leads to Service
    Paying It Forward
    Giving "As I Am Able" Leads to Self-fulfillment

9.1 FROM PASSIVE INDIFFERENCE TO ACTIVE PARTICIPATION

TO BECOME A GIVER

So, why should we give? How do we create a culture of giving?

PLAYBOOK EXERCISE

- How would you answer the "why give" question?
- Name three people you think are generous and three you think are not generous.
- Write down three reasons why you think people do not like to give.
- Write down three reasons why you think people like to give.

NEXT STEP

- Determine the percentage of your money that you give away. Could you increase it by 1%? By 2%? Determine what you would like to do now and in the future.

MEMBERS OF THE HUMAN FAMILY

Our lives are the accumulation of social relationships: our family, our relatives, our teammates, our coaches and teachers, our school friends, our neighborhood and our nation.

We are part of what is now called the global village. As we become more aware, we realize that we are part of the whole human family, so in some sense all women are our sisters, and all men, our brothers.

One of the great challenges of growing up is in seeing the other person in this way. People of every nation and race and tribe begin by seeing themselves as somehow better than others.

This does not mean that we should not love our own people and our country best of all. We should love our own family heritage and our own country with a special feeling and devotion. Our family and our country are so much a part of us that they can give to us what no other relationship can give.

However, this love for our family and our country should open us up to the sacredness of all such relationships. We should be able to see that the love we share for our parents, brothers and sisters is the same as is shared by others everywhere, for their loved ones. We are poor citizens if we cannot see that others surely feel the same warmth and loyalty and pride and devotion to their native lands as we do to ours. Our love of our land should lead us to universal empathy for those in other countries. A good family and a good neighborhood and a good town all complement and fulfill each other. So, too, nationalism and internationalism should complement each other and lead to a better world for all.

FINDING MEANING

Meaningful life comes not from seeing how much you can get, but from living for a worthy purpose. We have within ourselves that greedy self that occupies the first room in the house that is our soul. But as we grow older, we add on more and more rooms so that our soul can expand and include those larger selves that seek not for themselves but for others. As we continue to grow, we move more and more from "I" to "we," and from "mine" to "our."

PLAYBOOK EXERCISE

- Do you think we have a moral responsibility to others? If so, where, if anywhere, would you draw the line: local, national, international?
- In what ways can that be shown in your life?

NEXT STEPS

- What is an interest of yours that you have been thinking of becoming more involved in but to which you have not yet responded?
- What would be the first step for you to take?

THE MEANING OF CITIZENSHIP

This democracy that we cherish has as its underlying assumption a common ethic that we have inherited. The ethical assumption of our democracy has always been that we have a responsibility for one another, especially for those less fortunate. We're in this together. It is important to remember that the moral and ethical duty for the common good was inherited from our various traditions and assumed by people of all faiths and of no faith, as the sub-soil of our democracy.

PLAYBOOK EXERCISE

- What do you think it means to be a citizen or resident of this country? What are your civic duties as a citizen?
- What are the sources of the values that are most important to you in your life?

NEXT STEP

- Think about the values you cherish. Are they being taught and passed on, as they were to you? Consider what you can do about that. Will you?

9.2 DISCOVERING THE POWER OF GIVING

COMPASSION LEADS TO SERVICE

We come together and work for the common good because we care. To work for the common good—to live out that civic responsibility we have as citizens—leads us to join together for countless activities and good works. We fight against cancer or other diseases; help out at an art museum, a symphony hall, or a sports stadium; build a home for a homeless person; respond to natural disaster cleanup or a neighbor's dying parent, all because we care.

PAYING IT FORWARD

We join together because we know we can make a difference and because we know that others have come before us and made things possible for us.

And so, we must look inside ourselves. We must determine that our life will make a difference. We cannot look for a life of ease and isolation as if the only reason we are here is to see how much we can get! We must let our hearts be open to the difficulties, the struggles, the pain of others, so that the empathy we feel may shape us, move us, and lead us to greater caring. We must be willing to walk with others and share their burdens so that we may lighten their load and give hope to their despair.

In our daily lives we must do more than random acts of kindness. We must let the fabric of our lives reflect and radiate a desire to make this a better world. In other words, we must live fully and completely. If we live life, love life, and give life, we will be alive as never before. Most importantly, we'll all have a better community and a better world.

PLAYBOOK EXERCISE

- Who has "paid for you" and helped you become the person you are today?

- What problems in your community or in the world have you responded to? What is it that blocks you from responding more often?

NEXT STEP

- Write out three community-based goals for yourself for the coming year. They should be three goals that will help you make a difference in the lives of those nearby or far away.

GIVING "AS I AM ABLE" LEADS TO SELF-FULFILLMENT

"As I am able" is something that each person must define for himself or herself. It may mean giving up one Saturday morning—or many. It may mean giving up one dollar—or many dollars. The life that flows into us in innumerable ways must also flow out of us. The important thing is that we have a common understanding: We all have a responsibility for the betterment of our world, and that responsibility begins with small steps and small actions.

Some people are not used to giving money away. But two things are true: Giving helps the giver, and giving helps the receiver. Whenever we give a gift, we feel better than before. Whenever we respond to a need, we feel better. Why? Because we become more of a person, and our sense of self, of who we are, is developed. In other words, rather than just trying to live alone and selfishly get all we can for ourselves, when we reach out and respond to our neighbors in need, we find our own lives enriched.

When we respond and reach out, we grow and become more than we were before. We also have a sense of accomplishment, which will lead us to do additional things in the future.

The goal we are always working toward is that of developing a generous heart and a generous spirit, which will result in asking ourselves if we are doing all we can and what the next step is.

Have you thought about the skills you have that would benefit others? We often think of "skills" as those superior abilities that only some have. In fact, we all have many skills: the skill of being a friend, of listening to another, of helping out by participating in a program or project, or of helping a younger person with a subject or sport. We all have many more skills to offer to others than we first recognize.

PLAYBOOK EXERCISE

- When have you felt the best as the result of serving others?
- What skills do you have? What would others say?
- How can you help others have a sense of responsibility for others?

NEXT STEPS

- What is the one thing you care most about in the world? What is the next step you can take to work on that issue?
- What other individuals or groups can you invite to join with you?